Heavenly Light

Heavenly Light

P.R. Wilkerson

Heavenly Light © Copyright 2023
P.R. Wilkerson

All rights reserved. No part of this book may be used or reproduced in any manner whatsoever without written permission of the author except in the case of brief quotations embodied in critical articles and reviews.

The information in this book is distributed as an "as is" basis, without warranty. Although every precaution has been taken in the preparation of this work, neither the author nor the publisher shall have any liability to any person or entity with respect to any loss or damage caused or alleged to be caused directly or indirectly by the information contained in this book.

Bible verses are used from the
Holy Bible King James Version
Regency Publishing House

First Edition
Paperback ISBN: 978-1-955541-26-8
Library of Congress Control Number: 2023914453

Published by FuzionPress
1250 E 115th Street
Burnsville, MN 55337
FuzionPress.com
612-781-2815

I give thanks to God for the inspiration that enabled me to put pen to paper and share these words with all who will read them.

I dedicate this book in loving memory of Jane Campbell, our sister in St. Stanislaus Women's Spirituality Group. God called Jane to her eternal home on May 17, 2023. Her compassion, wisdom, and spiritual strength will be missed by many. Without Jane telling me my poetry was a gift from God and meant to be shared, it would not be in the hands of others.

To my family, God bless you for all the love and kindness you share with me. An exuberant thank you to my niece, Kristin Carlson, for her technical support and patience. And a heartfelt thank you to all my sisters in St. Stan's Women's Spirituality Group for their encouragement and kind support; you are truly appreciated.

A special thank you goes to Mary Pat Miller for proofreading and emailing my manuscript to Fuzion Press. You gave my books the push they needed to get out the door.

Table of Contents

Seek and Find	11
Poetry	12
Poems	13
A Four-Leaf Clover	15
Fire, Fire	17
Family	21
In Loving Memory	22
Diamonds, Gems, and Jewels	23
Old Glory	25
Miles and Miles Apart	26
T.M.I.	27
Lost and Found	28
Pearls of Wisdom	29
What Would Jesus Do?	30
Your True Self	31
Hold On Tight	32
Tears	33
Thankful for Thee	34
Infinity	35
Different Strokes for Different Folks	36
Filled with Fun	37
Smile	38
A Merry Christmas	39
Laughter	41
Where's Mikey?	43
The Easter Basket	45
The Birthday Party	47

ST. STANISLAUS CHURCH	49
HOPE AND LOVE	50
THE WEDDING - HOLY MATRIMONY	51
GOD PROVIDES	52
WHISKERS IN THE SINK	53
A SEA SHELL WITH A HEART	55
CORNUCOPIA	56
A PEACEFUL PLACE	57
MY HOME AWAY FROM HOME	59
PRAY A LITTLE MORE	61
CATCH OF THE DAY	63
LUCKY TO BE	65
A HUMBLE RECIPE	66
HEAVENLY INDULGENCE	67
JUDGE NOT	68
INDIVIDUALITY	69
IF ONLY	70
INTERNAL STATE OF MIND – ODE TO UKRAINE	71
TO HELL AND BACK	72
WALK IN THE LIGHT	73
DREAMS	74
LATE AT NIGHT	75
SURREAL	76
BRIEF MOMENTS	77
SLEEPWALKING – SOMNAMBULISM	78
PRAYERS	79
ATONEMENT	80
FORGIVE ME	81
A PEACEFUL LOVING WAY	82

FOR ALL THE PONDERING POETS	83
HEAVENLY LIGHT	85
THE POETRY OF LIFE	87
TREKKING	89
MISERY	90
HAVE FAITH	91
I FOLLOW THE LORD	92
I LISTEN AND PRAY	93
FREE GIFTS	94
WHEEL OF FORTUNE	95
MEDITATION	96
LIFE CHALLENGES	97
ABUNDANT BLESSINGS	98
A PERFECT GIFT	99
GOD GUIDES US	100
REAP WHAT YOU SOW	101
PEACE OF MIND	103
GOD KNOWS	104
THE TRULY SPECIAL ONES	105
GUIDING LIGHT	106
A FRIEND'S PRAYER	107
A PACKAGE FOR MY FRIEND	109
MYSTERIOUS AND WONDERFUL WAYS	110
BLESSED	111
TRUE ECSTASY	113
WIND AND AIR	115
TREES	117
FLOWERS	119
RAIN SHOWERS	120

MILD WINTER BLUES	121
WEATHER	123
PAST, PRESENT AND FUTURE	125
UNCONDITIONAL LOVE	126
THEIR FUTURE	127
THE NEVER-ENDING DEBATE	128
WHY AGAIN-AND-AGAIN	129
CLOSER TO GOD	130
NOW IS THE TIME	131
WILLPOWER	132
TRUST IN LOVE	133
CONTEMPLATIVE MEDITATION	134
CHANGES	135
LOVE ONE ANOTHER	136
BELOVED ONES	137
HEAVENLY PLANS	138
THE LONG GOODBYE	139
PEACE AND JOY	141
ON HEAVEN'S DOOR STEP	142
THE INVISIBLE BECOMES VISIBLE	143
WELCOME HOME	145
ALL WILL BE REVEALED	147
ETERNITY	148
THE EVOLUTION OF A BOOK	149
NOTES ABOUT AUTHOR	150

Seek and Find

If you're curious, if you have an open-mind,
maybe you'll find something of value when you delve
deep inside.

Many years of experience, many years of life,
could be of some interest to all those willing to spend a
little time.

Values and opinions can be instilled in our minds.
But God-given wisdom and truths can be the blessings
we are all meant to find.

Poetry

I know not when, and I know not what they will be,
as it seems like a puzzle that appears to me.

I dare not question the outcome you see,
as it's a gift from God that's meant to be.

I'll share with others and, hopefully, the poems I write
will be a blessing from heaven for all to see.

Poems

Poems change as they grow; their life begins with a word then a few.
Hopefully they can be special for you.

Their depth can be great and shallow, too.
Their meanings will vary as they often do.

Hold them, read them, and search thoroughly through,
and maybe you'll find the one that's meant for you.

Josephine, mother of three, an Irish lass full of fun — a happy-go-lucky, special one

A Four-Leaf Clover

The luck of the Irish is special for me,
as I had a mother from a Celtic family.
The O'Donovans and O'Donnells fill our family tree;
Irish folks from the old country.

Our yard was filled with green clover and often you would see
A mother with her children down on their knees
hunting four-leaf clovers, and surely it would be
That the luck of the Irish would sustain our family.

In the beginning this was Alexander Ramsey's carriage house built 1884. In later years it became the apartment house my grandmother, Katherine, owned on that day where the fire burned so profound.

Fire, Fire

Each turn of the page feels like a beat of my heart. When telling this true story where do I dare start?

It feels like eons ago when it all began; one family's troubles from beginning to end.

The very first memory was being in my crib and it didn't seem like long before I was climbing in and out of it, again and again.

A mischievous toddler was I, and when I got together with my cousin, my friend, we found trouble, and that's how it all began.

Down on the floor was something new, so we picked it up trying to figure out what we could do.

One strike of the match and the flames flew high and to the closet ran he and I.

Firetrucks and firemen came from all around, and the sounds of their sirens roared throughout the town.

"Fire, fire!"

Plumes of smoke billowed out of the windows so high, someone noticed and rescued he and I.

Our apartment house was damaged, not burned to the ground. Thank God all were saved on that day so profound.

Katherine, mother of seven, Grandmother of 22; an independent woman loved by everyone.

Leonard, father of three, a social man was he, with love of nature you could plainly see.

Family

My dad, my father, my friend, someone I looked up to from the beginning to the end.
The lessons I've learned along the way are many, and I thank God when I pray.
His burdens were heavy when his health declined, as M.S. stole his strength, and he had to leave his family behind.

A wife and three young children were left alone, and it was not long before the mother of his children
became ill and passed on. Five separate ways for this family of five. Now facing challenges on where those left behind would reside.

Instilled at an early age was a strong faith in God and when they prayed for help;
it soon came along, and three young children then knew where they belonged.
Be thankful and grateful for those gifts from God,
and treasure them knowing he loves you and will guide you your whole life long.

In Loving Memory

The loss of a loved one is hard to bear,
even though we know they're
in heaven comforted by the Father
who welcomes his children with loving care.

We're thankful and grateful for all the years
our loved one was with us,
sharing our life filled with love, laughter and tears.

Diamonds, Gems and Jewels

The beauty of such multi-faceted jewels; not unlike God's children, when the light of love shines through.

The Lord is like a jeweler making each individual cut.
A life filled with blessings of hope, faith, and love.

How precious, how loved, more than any individual gem or jewel, are God's creations on Earth called his children, his heavenly-treasured gems and jewels.

Memorial Day at Fort Snelling Cemetery, Minneapolis, Minnesota

Old Glory

For the love of God and country, the red white and blue;
the flag honoring the military serving and protecting all
of us as they do.

God comfort the families grieving the loss of their loved
ones who
gallantly gave up their life in the line of duty
more bravely and heroically than most of us do.

Miles and Miles Apart

Even though you've lost your loved ones long, long ago, know that they're with you wherever you go.

You may be miles and miles apart but they're closer than you know,
as love fills your heart their memories are forever cherished in your soul.

T.M.I.

Too much information. Do you believe this, does this pertain to you?
Can you share with others that might have issues, too?
Have you been told not to do this, it will only harm you?

Trust in the Lord and pray fervently, then if you share with others,
remember we all have problems and knowing there's strength in numbers
we can pray together asking God to help us as only he can do.

Matthew 18:20 For where two or three are gathered together in my name, there I am in the midst of them.

Lost and Found

Long, long ago there was a time in my life I didn't want to exist.
I thought that I'd never be missed.

All desires were gone along with any possibilities of sleep.
Nothing mattered and nothing ever would. How could this happen to someone like me?

Slowly, so slowly, with the help of God, family and friends,
I found I was needed, thank God and Amen!

Pearls of Wisdom

We all wonder why when things go astray;
was there something we could have done or changed in
a different way?

And if we hit bottom and dwell in the dark,
it can be then when we're broken apart
that those pearls of wisdom fill our heart.

Trust in God and his heavenly light.
Walk with him, morning noon and night.

What Would Jesus Do?

Sometimes we're talkative and really don't know why.
Other times we're sensitive and need time to process
and maybe cry.

If we can reflect and listen a little more,
we might just help others if only we pause before
dismissing someone's feelings and moving on to only
ours.

Your True Self

Who are you; what is this all about;
why all the changes, have you figured something out?

Trust in your instincts and follow your heart;
prayers have been answered. God is showing you your true self.

Be thankful and grateful knowing the truth
and recognizing all the blessings God has given to you.

Hold On Tight

If you're drowning in an overwhelming lake of tears,
and a splash of humor suddenly appears,

hold on tight when that life line is near,
as God is pulling you up with a little bit of cheer.

Tears

Tears of sorrow, tears of joy;
we all experience them more than once in a while.
Trust in God to show us the way
and guide us through our sorrowful days.

Share with others fun-filled times,
all God's blessings keep in mind.
Tears of joy will flow one day,
trust in God as you kneel down to pray.

Thankful for Thee

Thank you, dear God, for today,
in each and every way;
thank you, dear God, for tomorrow,

I pray there will be no sorrow.
Whatever you choose for me,
I'll always be thankful for thee.

Ecclesiastes Chapter 7:3 Sorrow is better than laughter: for by the sadness of the countenance the heart is made better.

Infinity

The Great I Am. The alpha and omega, there's no beginning there's no end.
It's unlimited, boundless, eternal, unconditional love.

Thank God for the most precious gift he has given to all his children;
nothing more could anyone ask for than God's infinite perpetual,
everlasting, never-ending, totally unconditional love.

Psalm Chapter 46:10 Be still, and know that I am God.

Different Strokes for Different Folks

I'm not stoic, I'm not a stiff shirt.
When I think something's silly and funny,
I'll be one who laughs first.

So, if you lack a sense of humor and jokes elude you,
remember others are doing their best to be happy,
and that's not meant to offend you.

Filled with Fun

Whether a poem is sweet and spicy
or cold and icy,
you'll know it's just right
when it satisfies with delight.

So, go no further, just linger a while,
and if it brings a smile
you've found the one
that's filled with fun
and can be shared with everyone.

Smile

If you're watching paint dry, grass grow,
and turtles racing, maybe your life could be a little slow.
And maybe skydiving, horse racing, or running the three-minute mile
doesn't interest you at all; but if you're willing to search for what pleases you
your life could become more fulfilling and joyful if only you forge ahead and put on your smile.

A Merry Christmas

The house is all decorated; the lights are twinkling so bright,
soon it will be Christmas, the holiest of nights.

The children are excited, the mangers in sight.
Baby Jesus is born we'll celebrate tonight.

The carolers are singing, the house is filled with joy.
The church bells are ringing; we'll be on our way,
headed for the celebration on this Merry Christmas Day.

Carmen and Calvin with the sound of a smile and the color of joy

Laughter

The color of joy, the sound of a smile;
children will show you if you watch them for a while.

Rosie-pink cheeks and high- pitched laughter;
what pleasures they bring as they play faster and faster.

The gifts they share for all to see
are blessings from heaven for you and me.

Mikey just looking at me

Where's Mikey?

Early one morning it was later than I thought.
Calling kitty, kitty before I rushed out the door,
not one meow was heard so I'll look a little more.

Cats are independent and do as they please,
and I can't find Mikey as I'm crawling down on my knees.

There in my bed nonchalantly as could be
was my cat Mikey all comfortable and cozy just looking at me.

Corinne, a talented young pianist and budding artist.

The Easter Basket

A vintage porcelain doll and her new bunny too,
are saying Easter prayers for a new friend like you.

You can draw and color to your hearts content
with all the supplies included, your time will be well spent.

We've got lots of candy in our basket for you
and plenty to share with others too.

Cousin Melanie's first birthday party; hail, hail the gang was all there.

The Birthday Party

Sisters, brothers and cousins of mine
gathered together for a joyful party of a special kind.
Treats will be served at the perfect time and songs will
be sung
wishing happy birthday to a sweet little one.

A day to be remembered many decades ago,
now thinking of loved ones, tugs on our heart strings
and fills us
with warm thoughts of blessings we shared so long,
long ago.

Stained glass windows at St. Stanislaus Church St Paul, Minnesota

St. Stanislaus Church

What visions, what insights, that opens our souls;
as we're gathered together in our church that feels so much like home.

The windows surround us; their colors abundantly flow,
as the sun shines through all our stained-glass windows.

The prayers, the homily, and holy communion, as God's love fills our souls
and opens our hearts with more blessings than the heavenly colors
of our church's stained-glass windows.

Hope and Love

A little bit of hope goes a long way.
A touch of true love we all long for each and every day.

Blessings from our Father we know they're on the way,
when we all gather together and kneel down to pray.

The Wedding – Holy Matrimony

The church is filled with prayerful blessings
as the couple stands side by side.
A bride and her groom now married.

Two hearts came together, true love blessed by the Divine.
Many guests gathered to witness a sacrament of the holiest kind.

We celebrate this joyful occasion with a toast to a man and his wife;
as the newlyweds are on their journey with a beautiful beginning to remember for the rest of their lives.

They are wished abundant blessings
filled with love, faith and joy, as they join together to experience
the wonders of an amazing, truly special, long and loving life.

God Provides

Pay it forward have no regrets;
life is a blessing. Mindfulness is truly what's best.
Speak from the heart, helping others,
while paying attention and doing it with kindness.

Gifts are all around us; focus on giving to others
knowing God provides all his children with what they
need next.

Whiskers in the Sink

How many times I've told you; how many times have I said;
they're disgusting and unsightly and I really do dread
all those whiskers in the sink.

One day it happened,
there's no more whiskers in the sink;
just a shiny porcelain bowl and you'd think
I'd be real happy with that clean empty sink.

But the truth of the matter is it's you that I'm missing;
I hadn't anticipated how soon I'd lose my partner,
the one who left whiskers in the sink.

So, if you love your partner and he loves you in return,
forget about the small things and focus on what really matters,
because that emptiness can happen suddenly with no love in return.

The unexpected; the unusual sea shell bound for me

A Sea Shell with a Heart

The unexpected, the unusual, can appear
when our heart needs a little cheer.

While missing a loved one and wishing they were here,
Suddenly a sea shell washed up on the shore so very
clear.

A prayer had been said for what happened here, believing that sea shell,
with the shape of a heart in its middle, meant my loved one was still very near.

Cornucopia

The horn of plenty with morsels of delight.
The heavenly manna, the sustenance for life.
The fuel for energy, the colors so bright.

The pleasures that sustain us consume,
and be thankful as you're sharing with others
the gifts that surround us each day of our life.

A Peaceful Place

Thank you, dear God, for I've seen what is here;
the peace in this place is always so near.

For Lindsay, Alice, Mary, Raylene, Mary Pat,
Linda, Lisa, Bobbie, L.B., Patty, Deb, Jill, Jane, and Jean,

and all the sisters who have shared this space.
Please keep peace in our hearts till we meet here next spring.

Retreat at St. John's Abbey, Lake Sagatagan
Collegeville, Minnesota

My Home Away from Home

As I open the door and sit on the bed,
it feels like I'm home all over again.

To look out the window and see such heavenly sights,
nothing more could I ask for, not ever in this life.

The wind dancing through the tree tops, the branches swaying with delight,
as the lake ripples with gentle movement,
you'd think it was all planned for my pleasure on this Monday so bright.

I'll enjoy every moment and when day turns to night,
I'll thank God for the treasures he surely has brought.

We know our Father heard us, then we pray a little more

Pray A Little More

The silence in the room and the peace in this place;
where so many prayers have been uttered,
God knows we long for his grace.

All the doors begin to open, all our strength we regain,
as our Father blesses us we no longer feel any pain.

And before this night is over, our hearts fill with joy,
and we know our Father heard us then we pray a little more.

Pencil drawing by Patty

Catch of the Day

Look and see, then do your best;
fish are waiting to fill your nest.

A swift flying bird looked down at the lake,
looking for dinner, hardly ever making a mistake.

She dove in the water as she saw her prey;
and caught that big fish, then flew far away.

Snowflakes gently land on the branches where the sticky pine needles are holding on tight

Lucky To Be

What more could I ask for; how lucky can I be;
to look out the window and see all I see?

The bright whiteness of the sky, the darkness of the
trees,
and the slight movement of the winds as the snowflakes
gently land
on the branches where the sticky pine needles are holding on tight.

Then a flock of birds flying over the frozen lake
patiently wait for spring to finally break.

A Humble Recipe

- A pat on the back
- An encouraging word
- A wink of the eye
- A glimpse of a smile
- A much-needed prayer

When God's gifts are shared with others it lightens our load,
squashes our fears, brings us together and humbles us so.

Heavenly Indulgence

A poem can be a recipe from heaven when you add all the ingredients with prayer.

- Two handfuls of love.
- A pound or two of paper.
- A generous portion of words.
- A pen to spread the words out.

Gently stir in love. Top with warm thoughts.
Add sprinkles of consideration, and say a little prayer.

Voila; Will serve many with a full measure of emotions that fills their hearts with joy.

Judge Not

If you have gray hair, crow's feet, a pot belly and a number of aches and pains,
there's no need to worry as God loves you just the same.

Judge not your sisters and brothers whatever their condition may be;
love one another and heed God's message for we know it's what was meant to be.

Individuality

We are all different, we are all alike. It's okay to want to be the center of attention,
It's okay to want to blend in and not stand out.

To respect our differences and accept
each other as we are. This is how God created us all equal, all equally loved.
Thank God for this gift of unconditional love.

If Only

When life becomes so mysterious and you wonder what it is all about;
all of a sudden it comes to a screeching halt.

You can't go any further without some Divine help;
just know your Father is with you, if only you would ask for his help.

Internal State of Mind – Ode to Ukraine

Comfort those around you, for it matters not our material surroundings,
as heaven can be found in a hell of a place. And hell can be found in a heavenly place.

Ask God to guide you; follow your heart and pray.

When loved ones surround you, it becomes a beautiful and peaceful day.

To Hell and Back

A son of Satan's is not for me.
I met someone like him unfortunately. His words were smooth as he complimented me,
and the gifts he brought flowed generously. I went with him trustingly not knowing what could happen to me.

Days of hell were about to come, headed my way from this evil one.
Time stood still as he cornered me in a room, so dark, dank and lacking of love unfortunately.
If only I could escape as this evil was thick and suffocating me.

Strength from within bolstered me and I escaped miraculously.
Years now long ago have gone by, and I thank God
I've never again met anyone like that guy.

Walk In The Light

If you've touched the darkness and now you're walking in the light,
just know your Father is with you when you pray morning noon and night.

Thank him for the protection as he guides you through your life;
never forget how much he loves you as your walking in the light.

Dreams

When you're dreaming in the middle of the night,
how do you stop nightmares when you know not where you're at?

You want to have pleasant dreams and sleep restfully through the night,
but when they become night terrors, oh God, they're such a fright.

Even though you pray most of the time,
there's no way of predicting what will be on your mind.

So, I'll do my best to think pleasant thoughts, right before bedtime,
And, hopefully, good dreams will enter into my mind.

Late At Night

The wind howls and the shutters bang,
late at night on my windowpane.

Is someone there, I do exclaim,
pounding on my windowpane?

Only then and not before,
I'm wondering if I locked my door.

Time stood still while I waited for someone
I thought would surely barge in and scare me more.
Should I rush to the door and bolt it tighter than before?

There's no need to hurry now as my eyes open and I realize like before;
it's all a dream I've had and nothing more.

Surreal

It seemed like reality even though it was a dream, about the past that came to me.
I was holding your hand as I kissed it so tenderly.

I thanked God for those moments that happened to me, as it brought us together like we used to be.

When I awoke, I felt the touch of a cool breeze on my face,
then a tear was shed wishing I was once more in your loving embrace.

Brief Moments

How precious those moments in the past were for me.
If only I could go back and see my loved ones that are no longer with me.
To hold them, cherish them, and never leave them for all of eternity.

This is what dwells deep down inside of me
and comes to the surface when night falls and sleep comes,
then dreams unfold that are holding those precious memories.
Thank God for those brief moments. It's a glimpse of the future unfolding before me.

Sleepwalking – Somnambulism

Anxiety and tensions, cause and effect,
cause and effect, how do we know which one is correct?

Toss and turn, toss and turn, here we go walking again and again.
Let it go, let it go, at this time there are really no answers for us to know.

Prayers

A morning prayer. Forgive me dear God for all of my stress.
Thank you, dear God, for I am truly blessed.

A nightly prayer. Thank you, dear God for all of my stress.
Forgive me, dear God, for not recognizing how I was blessed.

Atonement

A furrowed brow, a mean scowl, a cross word and vile anger erupts.
Be penitent, take deep breaths, count to ten.

Say a prayer and give it to God, then let it go.
Be patient, have hope; smiles will reveal when God heals.

Forgive Me

Why did I do that, what did I say; will you forgive me for being that way?
Can an Act of Contrition heal the pain of today?
I'm down on my knees Lord, please forgive me I pray.

You did what you did and said what you said;
you asked for forgiveness before you went to bed.

You awoke in the morning and said your prayers,
hoping God heard you as you rushed down the stairs.

A new day is beginning; you'll go on your way,
being more careful to watch what you say.

A Peaceful Loving Way

Trust your Father to guide you when you kneel down to pray.
Setting examples for others can be the Godly way.

Help one another as you travel throughout your days, knowing we're meant to be together in peaceful loving ways.

For All the Pondering Poets

If deep within you feel there is a need for one more,
will you write it and share it with others as you did before?

Prayers and meditation, asking God to guide the way;
writing meaningful messages for others in a spiritual,
loving, and poetic way.

Specificity and simplicity are words used today,
hoping others find your poetry encouraging and helpful
at the end of their day.

Close your eyes and wish upon a star knowing it's Gods light shining from afar

Heavenly Light

The miracles and powers that created such awe-inspiring wonders so near and so far,
from the Pacific to the Atlantic and south to the seas,
then north to Alaska will surely please.

Now move onward; look upward and gaze upon the mesmerizing stars,
the galaxies, solar systems, universe and more,
as God's heavenly light reflects beyond even Mars.

Take time to ponder and wish upon a star,
realizing how blessed we truly are.

Niagara Falls view from Canada

The Poetry of Life

Poetry in life will always be many of God's blessings for
you and me.
Gifts of love and nature are beautiful to see
and are meant to be shared with others for all of
eternity.

Thank him once and thank him again,
knowing he loves you forever and ever, Amen.

Lake Sagatan, Collegeville, Minnesota

Trekking

The singing of the birds, the scurrying of the squirrels,
the splashing of the geese as the turtle sits on his log.

We hike along the lake shore enjoying the warm and sunny day;
what more could two crones ask for as they go merrily along their way?

Misery

Today is a miserable day, sneezing, coughing, trying to sleep it all away. All energy is depleted, I feel like one of the departed.

Oh, woe is me, can't write poetry when you're sick I see. Now it's back to bed for me.

Have Faith

As life unfolds God shows us the way;
trust in him all of your days.

Challenges will come and choices must be made;
have faith knowing he will guide you as you kneel down
to pray.

Some troubles are blessings in disguise,
as they teach us compassion on how to humbly survive.

Be thankful and grateful at the end of day,
knowing you spread love as you went on your way.

I Follow the Lord

Intuition or premonition,
which one could it be?
Does it really matter;
I guess we'll soon see.

Happy go-lucky, it matters not to me;
as I trust the Lord and follow him,
for that's what truly is meant to be.

I Listen and Pray

Suggestions are not set in stone.
Even though we may have had troubles of our own
that mimic others, it does not mean we are able
to solve issues that are theirs alone.

The road is paved with good intentions, as God knows.
And sometimes attentive listening and heartfelt prayers
for those going through difficulties could be the only answers
that can help them recover from their downtrodden
woes and cares.

Free Gifts

A walk in the sun with a loved one can be
one of the most pleasurable experiences in life for me.

The simplest things seem to be that God has given us many
highly treasured gifts that are truly free.

Wheel Of Fortune

The wheel of fortune is a game for me.
Spin the wheel; it's fun you'll see.

Pat and Vanna will guide you through
each spin of the wheel; it's easy to do.

Guess the letters then solve the puzzle;
collect your winnings and go on your way,
giving thanks to God for this lucky day.

Meditation

Trust in God to guide the way
when we're longing for peaceful days.

Set aside time for solemn prayer;
meditation could hold the answers there.

Focus on the Lord and quiet your mind,
being thankful to him for all that you find.

Life Challenges

Poetry and puzzles are the same to me,
as they are a challenge to solve, you'll see.
A piece of a puzzle placed here or there,
until it fits, is only fair.

A word of a poem can only go
in the right place until we know it's just so.

Challenges in life seem to be so much like puzzles and poetry.
Make the right choices and then we'll see
poetry and puzzles in life can be miracles from God for you and me.

Abundant Blessings

Reach out to one another and see what you will find.
God's given us many blessings of an abundant, special kind.

The words we share together are surely meant to be,
for there some of the blessings from God for you and me.

A Perfect Gift

A day of silence is not hard for me,
as I live alone very quietly.

Not one word was spoken today;
hopefully tomorrow it will be another way.

I can phone a friend or visit the store,
surely something will be said and I'll be quiet no more.

Silence is golden, many say,
and I can agree in a number of ways.

A kind word or a few can be golden too,
when shared with others like we often do.

Meditation and conversation, when balanced, can be
a perfect gift to share for all of humanity.

God Guides Us

Ribbons and ribbons of black highways wrapped around the fields of yellow corn.
Miles and miles of traveling until the setting of the golden sun.

Rest and relaxation at the end of our day.
Prayers filled with anticipation as God guides us lovingly along our way.

Reap What You Sow

There's beauty, there's kindness, there's love in our hearts.
When we're together it's as though we were never apart.

God blesses his children wherever they are.
Sow seeds of kindness, harvest bushels of love.
Then thank God for the goodness he sends down from above.

Lisa, Patty and Linda on a walk in nature

Peace of Mind

I start with a prayer and then pen in hand;
words will be expressed with the best intentions as a plan.

A walk in nature brings peace of mind,
many other benefits are yours to find.

Surprise, surprise for all to see,
life can be an open book filled with meaningful poetry.

God Knows

The brightness of your smile,
the sparkle in your eyes,
no one will forget you,
not even if you're gone for a very long while.

The joy that you bring, the compassion you share,
fills our hearts with more love and God knows how much we care.

The Truly Special Ones

Happy are those with good thoughts on their mind,
thinking of others most of the time.

Sharing and caring you'll always find
they're doing good deeds with love on the line.

Smiling, laughing and enjoying life.
Graceful, generous, honest and kind.

They're truly special; thank God we met them
as they're a blessing to find.

Guiding Light

Sometimes we can't see what's right in front of our eyes and we may wonder why.

Then all of a sudden, a door begins to open and a light is shining so bright
as God is beginning to reveal all our blessings with his heavenly light.

Be thankful and grateful for all the experiences in our life, knowing God is with us, he's truly our heavenly guiding light.

A Friend's Prayer

A friend is a gift that everyone needs.
We care for each other as is meant to be.

They know us and see us for who we really are.
We depend on each other, two together we're stronger by far.

Nothing more could one ask for than a special friend,
a blessing from the beginning that never ends.
Thank God forever and ever, Amen.

Angels are God's messengers

A Package for My Friend

Where do I mail this, how will I get this to you?
Now that you're in heaven,
can you get this message that's lovingly meant for you?

The words are from my heart, the poems I'm sending to you;
God only knows the distance that this package has to travel before it reaches you.

Until we meet in heaven, I'll be thinking of you,
and thanking God for our friendship as truly friends would do.

Mysterious and Wonderful Ways

There's no rhyme or reason for wanting to know,
why God works his miracles in mysterious and wonderful ways.

Trust in God to guide us, and question not his ways,
for ours is but to follow each and every day.

Blessed

Are they angels; are they miracles; are they gifts from
God the family that loved me and provided a home?
The clown who found me at the circus when I was crying and lost all alone.

The fireman who rescued me from the closet as the fire
burned all around.
The priest who pulled me up when my spirits were
down.
The women's group that encouraged me and took me
into their fold.

Angels, miracles, or gifts from God,
whatever they are I'm thankful, grateful, and blessed by
far.

Sunset, Island Lake, Park Rapids, MN

True Ecstasy

The joy and excitement in life can be some of the simplest things we see.
When we become aware and thank God for opening our eyes so lovingly;

it transforms our visions of nature more honestly.
We now know what he has created is true ecstasy.

Thank God for all the wind and air that only the greatness of his love can share.

Wind and Air

The beauty of the bends in the trees from the blowing of the wind.
The playful tickling of the leaves at the slightest movement of the wind.

The life-saving energy the windmills store as the wind churns and turns throughout the day.
The heavenly sounds of the choir as they sing holy songs and pray.

Thank God for all the wind and air
that only the greatness of his love can share.

One of God's creations, so narrow, green and tall, on the shore line of Lake Sagatagan, Collegeville Minnesota

Trees

Just outside my window stands one of God's creations,
so narrow, green and tall. Where will it lead you as
you're mesmerized with it all; only your imagination
can tell you if you're willing to take the risk, knowing
you won't fall,

remember it's your imagination that can take you to all
the places God's created; if your
bodies are physically unable to stand such a long haul.

Pink peonies with an intoxicating scent

Flowers

The stems, leaves and petals so perfectly formed.
A rainbow of colors with intoxicating scents.
The large, small and massively abundant varieties of all;

Thank God for those blessings chosen with love.
Nothing more could we ask for as we're surrounded
by these gifts of nature all given with heavenly love.

Rain Showers

Oh, the wonderful sights and sounds of the drizzling, sprinkling, now pouring-down rain.
As it waters the trees and gardens, then blesses the earth's heavenly grounds.

To see, to hear, to know the gifts we are given are all around.
It's a matter of accepting and thanking God for the bounties
he so lovingly, wisely and generously is sending down.

Mild Winter Blues

Do you ever get an inkling that all you want to do is go to bed,
pull the covers up over your head,
close your eyes and just wait till spring arrives?

Do not despair; don't even give it a care. We all know what's best.
If you really need a rest,
take your time you'll be just fine.
A short nap will do and, in the end, you won't be so blue.

So, close your eyes and you can surmise
a much-needed rest was truly what was best.

Minnesota's blanket of snow; children love it, cold weather and all

Weather

There are blessings of blue skies, sunshine and warm breezes we all love so. Then rain showers. May flowers and heavenly rainbows.

Winter will come and snowflakes will fall; children will love them, cold weather and all.
Be prayerful and careful as you go on your ways, thanking God for good weather all of your days.

Bridge on a path at St. John's Abbey Collegeville, Minnesota

Past, Present and Future

The building blocks of the past are the bridge to the future.
The only way to live in the now is to recognize and open our eyes,
accepting this gift from God; known as the present given to us before our future.

Unconditional Love

Truth, honesty and the purest forms of unconditional love
are found in the eyes of your littlest ones.

A gentle touch from the tiniest of hands,
depending on us is one of God's heavenly plans.

Each smile they share no one can deny;
they capture our hearts in a blink of an eye.

Their Future

The children; their future; what truths can be told. Who among us are contemplating about what kind of life they'll have if all the resources are gone.

Children deserve a clean, healthy environment, now and when they're adults with a family of their own.

Take care, do no harm, save their future before all the resources are gone.

The Never-Ending Debate

Youth has more strength. Age has more knowledge. Youth has better health.

Age has more awareness. Youth has more energy. Age has more experience.

Youth has a longer life. Age has a grateful life. Youth will age and the never-ending

debate will start all over again, without an end.

Why, Again and Again

Mass shootings. How can we stand by and lose our loved ones; our children, our family, our friends.
God, help us stamp out this evil invading our country, over and over again.

What questions, what answers, what actions will stop this horror and terror from torturing the minds of those losing their children, their family and friends?

Almighty God, we're praying and pleading for help to rid us of this vile evil. Amen.

Closer to God

Earthquakes, fires, monsoons and haboobs.
Blizzards, pandemics, many losses, then heartbreaks ensue.

The more challenges, situations, and ramifications we go through;
we're down on our knees Lord, with many prayers offered to you;
hoping and succeeding in being stronger, wiser, and closer to God as we do.

Now is the Time

Global warming and climate change
all over the world seems so strange.
The loss of homes on frozen shores
where polar bears roam will be no more.

National parks, such as Yellowstone,
were closed to the public, when the melting snow
washed away bridges and homes.

The heat is increasing across the globe as the ozone
is shrinking; we could all be in trouble before we know.

Pay attention and be willing to start;
changes can be made as there's still time now
if we all just do our part.

Willpower

No matter how determined we are to solve serious issues all alone,
willpower needs more than a voice of its own.

Meditation and deep conversation, as God's spirit fills our souls
and conquers all those fears, willpower, the ego, can't do on its own.

Trust in Love

Come hell or high waters, we'll gather together searching for safe places.
Sanctuaries, churches and more; when the whirlwind of turbulence,
violence, storms, unspeakable things are knocking on our doors.

Prayers will be offered, an evil will be conquered
as God restores the love that was lost by those moments of fear.
Fear not that evil, trust in God's love.

The day will come, we'll live as one
and joy will erase all the sadness that took place
as hearts heal and God's true love is revealed.

Contemplative Meditation

Some say my books are inspirational; some say they're spiritually based.
Yet others say my memoirs in reality are true poetry, verse by verse.

It matters not the genre or what title truly comes first.
Connecting with others, then looking within and knowing truth,
is God's inspiration; the beginning that never ends.

Changes

To look at something through another person's eyes
can be a blessing and a wonderful surprise.

To see one another in a different way
can make night time feel like the middle of the day.

If you have tunnel vision and you need a change,
pray for an open mind even though it seems so strange.

You're never too old to learn new ways,
just keep on trying till the end of your days.

Love One Another

Nature doesn't worry it; it goes with the flow.
The birds in the sky and the critters below
follow their instincts and know which way to go.

As God's children we trust him, as his spirit fills our soul.
We learn to love one another and all he's created,
sharing his blessings wherever we go.

Beloved Ones

God so loved the world that he gave his only son
to redeem all his children, each and every one.

How cherished, how blessed to be loved by the Holy One,
as we're called his children, each and every one.

St. John Chapter 3:16 For God so loved the world, that he gave his only begotten son, that whosoever believeth in him should not perish, but have everlasting life.

Heavenly Plans

The fragility of the aged can be difficult to see,
when experienced by a loved one that
was once as young and strong as you and me.

Always be willing to help when you can.
Hoping they'll realize and welcome you
as one of God's heavenly plans.

The Long Good Bye

How many times you've thought about it;
how many times you've tried
to unlock all those memories
that are locked deep down inside.

They say not to worry,
not ever even try, to recover all those things you've lost,
not really knowing why.

No one knows the answers or could tell me why,
so, I won't bother asking; I'll just close my eyes
and say good bye.

Sunset at Lake Michigan, Wisconsin

Peace and Joy

As we come together and trust in God, day by day, each step we take, truth and grace will light the way.

The love of God is filled with peace and joy.
All God's blessings we'll share with others and truly enjoy.

On Heaven's Doorstep

A wave of a hand, a glimpse of a smile,
no one has seen you for a very long while.

Will they remember the last time we were together,
the closeness we felt; the hugs we shared as we laughed
and cried?

No one will know until that day God calls you home
from so far away.

The Invisible Becomes Visible

You take a step back before you step out,
if you want to know what your whole life was about.

Seeing what matters and knowing the truth;
trusting in God and following through.

Conquering fears as true love is revealed.
The Holy Spirit is within and now steps out,
and you are no longer wondering what your whole life
was about.

Statue of a welcoming Jesus at St. Stanislaus Church

Welcome Home

The mysterious, mystical and magical; some of the most unexplainable things.
People are asking, not knowing the answers. What could have happened?
Are they miracles; are they gifts from God? Does anyone really know?

Maybe in time truth will be told and all will be well. The unexplainable will be known.
No questions will be asked and the mysterious, mystical and magical miracles
will be common when God welcomes us all to his heavenly home.

As we're closer to heaven our souls will soar high

All Will Be Revealed

I am a senior citizen, but I'm young at heart.
With so many blessings where do I start?

The sun in the morning, the stars at night,
my friends surround me, so much love fills my heart.

A life God has given me I'll know why,
when I'm closer to heaven my soul will soar high.

Eternity

To gain, to absorb, to fulfill the unquenchable desire, to acquire
more and more spiritual enlightenment of God's freely given wisdom
and truths along life's path to eternity.

Once the search begins our spiritual growth expands.
The journey may be long and slow or short and swift.
And in the end the beginning begins without an end.
Spiritual life is near as eternity is here.

Corinthians 16:44 It is sown a natural body: it is raised a spiritual body.

The Evolution of a Book

Page by page and day by day or night by night,
God guides me on what to write.

Just like a sculpture working the clay,
I can feel my book evolving and taking form in a certain way.

Soon I'll know when my work is done
and, God-willing, this book will be read by many a one.

NOTES ABOUT THE AUTHOR

Patty grew up in northern California and now resides in a cottage in the suburbs of St. Paul, Minnesota. She retired from Children's Home Society of Minnesota and now spends time with family and friends in St. Stanislaus Women's Spirituality Group.

She completed her first book, *Heart to Heart*, in December 2021. Once again, she put pen to paper with the inspiration from God and encouragement from family and friends to complete *Heavenly Light*. Being blessed with a long life, she has had many challenges, awakenings, and miracles. She is grateful for them all.

She believes that when this book touches someone's life in a positive way, by the grace of God it has accomplished what it was meant to do.

Printed in the USA
CPSIA information can be obtained
at www.ICGtesting.com
LVHW071942270923
759507LV00008B/115